#VERYFAT
#VERYBRAVE

#VERYFAT
#VERYBRAVE

The Fat Girl's Guide to Being #Brave and Not a Dejected, Melancholy, Down-in-the-Dumps Weeping Fat Girl in a Bikini

NICOLE BYER

Photographs by Kim Newmoney

Andrews McMeel
PUBLISHING®

SPECIAL THANKS

to synthetic wigs, Beyoncé, Kim Newmoney (who I truly adore and couldn't have done this without), and everyone who let me take a picture at their place of work. Everyone from the nice man at the front desk of the Palm Springs Hotel to the ride operators at the Santa Monica Pier. Without these kind people, I wouldn't have been able to take pictures in almost 100 different bathing suits, most of which I already owned. Oh! I gotta thank Alison Rich, who once said I should turn my Instagram bikini pictures into a book: thank you, Alison! I should also thank Sasheer, JoÚ, Matteo, and anyone else I've asked to take a picture of me in a bikini.

So okay, LET'S GET THE FUCK TO IT! I assume you picked up this book because you know who I am. If you don't know, that's okay; buy the book, then google me, in that order. Maybe you picked it up because you are a fat woman looking to find your #bravery, or you are a curious little creature wondering how a fat woman could ever be #brave in a bikini and not want to kill herself. Or you're a person who hates fatties and you're buying this book as a joke. Good, I'll take your money. I don't need to be liked to get paid.

Whatever the reason you picked it up, thank you. Thank you for reading this little intro. Now I'm going to ask you a favor for reading this far . . . please, please, please for the love of God follow through and buy it. Please don't share this book; make your friends buy their own copies. If you buy the book I will give you all my tricks and tips on how to be the #bravest bitch in your city, town, county, or municipality. Let's get real: even if you're sitting on the floor of a Barnes & Noble and reading it for free (that's what I used to do to kill time when I lived in New York and was too poor to take the subway home then go out again), I will still give you the tips and tricks, because you gamed the system, and I applaud you.

Real quick, I just wanna tell you why I wrote this book. I wanted to write a book about fat ladies—because I am one. Not curvy, not plus-size, not big-boned, not fluffy, not phat. I'm FAT. I am a fat lady who loves wearing bikinis. Which is #verybrave in our culture today. I realized this was #brave when I saw other fat women posting pictures in bikinis on Instagram, and people in the comments section went wild and were using that word: "brave." I never thought wearing an article of clothing that everyone wears to swim or sunbathe in was "brave," but as my dad always said, "If someone says something more than once in Instagram comments, it must be true." He died in 2008 so it's wild that he was truly so ahead of his time.

Now, I've come to embrace being #veryfat #verybrave and I want to help other women/people be #brave too. It took me a long time to be #brave, and I don't want others to have to wait. I want a little fat girl to see this book and feel better about herself. Before anyone says it: no, I am NOT glorifying an unhealthy lifestyle. I'm purely asking people to just be okay with how they currently look. I'm asking for people to leave others alone in regard to how they look, because it's not your fucking business. Also, I'm not promoting unhealthiness. If you're sick, please go to the doctor.

Now, that being said, truly anyone can wear a bikini. Alright, let the #bravery begin!

TIPS

Tips for Finding That Special Bikini That Will Make You #VeryFat and #VeryBrave

1. Go to a store, via public transportation, private transportation, or feet.
2. Find the bathing suit section (ask an employee where they keep the fat sizes—it may be in a dusty corner your fat eye can't spy).
3. Find a bikini.
4. Try it on (make sure you go to the fitting room, because if you don't, people may start screaming about indecent exposure or areolas or whatever).
5. Count your money or check your bank account. If you have no money, get a job, borrow from a friend, or rob a bank (but be peaceful about it), and return to step one. If you have money, go to the next step.
6. Go to the register and buy the bikini with cash or a card or, if you're feeling wild, a check.
7. Go home via public, private, or feet transportation.
8. Put on the bikini.
9. Live.

Tips for Finding That Special Bikini That Makes You #VeryFat and #VeryBrave for Millennials and/or Gen Zers

1. Go online and google "plus-size bikinis." (Don't yell, "WHERE ARE THE FAT-SIZE BIKINIS, GOOGLE?" because Google probably cannot hear you. If you need to yell and/or be listened to, use Siri or Alexa or something. Steps 2–5 will be done out loud if you use an internet assistant.)
2. Click on one of the results.
3. Find a bikini in your size.
4. Check your bank account. If you have no money, you can do an online scam or get a job of your choice, then go back to step one. If you have money, go to step five.
5. Order the bikini and make sure you click on the slowest free shipping option. Waiting a long time builds up the excitement.

6. Answer the door when the delivery person comes. If they just leave the package, then go to step eight.
7. Have a quick convo when you open the door, because they may be turned on by the story of your #bravery and want to fuck you. Do it. Or they could be a new friend.
8. Unbox and put the bikini on. If it fits, keep it. If not, return it to the store, then go back to the first step.
9. Live.

FYI, you may go through a full range of emotions during this process, and that's okay! You actually may hate what you see at first, because you're not used to it. You may think your tummy pokes out too much, but guess what? It fucking does when you're fully dressed. You may hate your arm jiggles, but they jiggle in sleeves. Your thighs are too large and in charge? Those are your thighs, why wouldn't you love them no matter how big they are or seem to you? Like anything in life, something new takes a hot-ass minute to get used to, so if you need to be #brave alone at home for a bit, that's okay. You can take your time.

#unsure

#sure

#blownawaybybravery

General Tips* for How to React to People in the World Who Respond Negatively, a.k.a. Frown Upon Your Bikini #Bravery

1. Smile and wave. Then blow them a kiss.
2. Say "You like what you see, daddy?" I'm not telling you to assume someone's gender, I'm just saying that this is a fun phrase, and if need be you can replace "daddy" with "mommy."
3. If they actually say something rude to you, you can respond, "Wow, I'm so sorry you don't have enough going on in your life that li'l fat ol' me wearing this upset you so much."
4. Talk loudly about how they are staring at you. People hate this. I do this a lot on airplanes. It's not my #bravery people take issue with but my being too loud on the phone. People like to turn around and glare at me to show how annoyed they are, and I'm all like, "Oh my God, this woman turned around and looked at me!" Nine times outta ten they don't want to do it again, because that's not the response they were looking for. They want me to be quiet, and that's not gonna happen, sister. I fucking love screaming and giggling.

Good Responses to Friends Who Want to Police Your Bikini Choice

1. "You're my friend, right, Tina? Don't get mad when I say this, but, like, lick my asshole, Tina. I'ma wear what I want."
2. "Hi Sherri, if you keep talking about what I should and shouldn't be wearing I may never hang out with you again, and, yes, Sherri, I realize I'm being dramatic, but so are you."
3. Keep asking "What?" until they give up.
4. Get new friends.

There are more specific tips on rude-ass people later.

What You Should Eat While Wearing a Bikini

1. Hamburger
2. Steak
3. Apples
4. Other fruits
5. Potatoes (in any iteration)
6. Mozzarella sticks
7. Cucumbers/eggplant/squash/anything phallic
8. Ravioli
9. The rest of the vegetables
10. Ice cream

That's it. Those are the only things you can eat while wearing a bikini. Sorry, I don't make the rules.

ACTIVITIES YOU CAN DO IN A BIKINI

1. Sleep
2. Sit
3. Walk
4. Dance
5. Shop
6. Sing
7. Sunbathe
8. Swim
9. Paint
10. Sneeze
11. Play a board game
12. Scratch your nose
13. Play the drums
14. Argue with your boyfriend
15. Listen to that Noah Cyrus song with Lil Xan (. . . I truly thought they would last.)
16. Eat a potato
17. Paint your toenails
18. Fly a kite
19. Have sex
20. Wave at a banana
21. Get on a trampoline
22. Jump on a trampoline
23. Get off a trampoline
24. Wave at a dog
25. Watch *Sex in the City*
26. Recite poetry to people who may or may not want to hear it
27. Ask your boss for a raise
28. Do cartwheels
29. Slap a disrespectful bitch
30. Hug your cousin
31. Watch *A Star is Born* for the tenth time
32. Wave at a plane
33. Take a midday nap
34. Sip alcohol
35. Guzzle alcohol
36. Throw away your alcohol, because you made a change in your life
37. Propose to your significant other on a cliff
38. Yell at a child crossing the street in unsafe conditions
39. Whisper your secrets to the wind
40. Pop popcorn for you and the neighborhood
41. Give your dog a bath
42. Turn lights off to save money
43. A split if you're flexible; a deep lunge if you aren't
44. Cry about a man who seemed to like you but ended up not liking you at all
45. Tell your mother about your dad's cheating
46. Drive your mother to a divorce attorney
47. High-five a teen rollerblading on the boardwalk
48. Learn the choreography to Beyoncé's 2018 Coachella performance

49. Complain about how you hate camping
50. Bounce a ball
51. Hold a baby
52. Have a real conversation with your dad about how he cheated on Mom
53. Yell at your dad's new girlfriend, "You'll never be my real mom!"
54. Row a boat
55. Skip in the middle of the road
56. Murder
57. Brush your hair
58. Shave your legs
59. Call your bestie
60. Break up with your significant other
61. Pet a flamingo
62. Ask if it's okay that you pet someone's flamingo
63. Army crawl into your neighbor's yard
64. Eat a taco
65. Hike
66. Say you want to hike and bail at the last minute
67. Do the hike and complain every seven minutes
68. Bake a cake . . . but be careful
69. Sixty-nine your partner
70. Get on a bus
71. Change a lightbulb
72. Eat bacon, but don't cook it in a bikini—the splatter will hurt
73. Eat candy
74. Give out candy on Halloween
75. Answer the door on Halloween and tell the youth you will give them no candy while eating candy
76. Call your best friend's other best friend
77. Garden
78. Vacuum your house
79. Frost a cake
80. Go to a movie
81. Wave at a child
82. Wave at a giraffe
83. Stretch
84. Yell at a child
85. Smoke weed
86. Ride a motorcycle
87. Hatch a plan with your twin sister to trade places and break up your dad and his new girlfriend
88. Slide down a waterslide
89. Play piano
90. Steal flowers from a yard
91. Tiptoe
92. Drink water
93. Watch *90 Day Fiancé*
94. Listen to podcasts like *Why Won't You Date Me?*, *Best Friends*, *90 Day Bae*, or *Drag Her!*
95. Tiptoe backward
96. Drop shit from a balcony
97. Dance in a parade
98. Braid your hair
99. Pick your nose
100. Find an alibi to cover up the murder you committed
101. Pole dance

102. Dance with no pole
103. Roll on the floor
104. Get a commercial driver's license
105. Make your bed
106. Sit in a hot tub alone
107. Drink tea with CBD oil
108. Turn and snap at a bitch and say, "I'm all that and a bag of chips!" (Why did we start saying that, and why did we stop?)
109. Sit behind someone and do pottery while the Righteous Brothers' "Unchained Melody" plays in the background
110. Learn karate
111. Blow kisses to a group of men
112. Eat a cookie
113. Eat another cookie
114. Finish the box of cookies
115. Text a friend
116. Phone a friend
117. Lock in your final answer
118. Feed a racoon
119. Create a comprehensive software product that can be used across multiple operating systems
120. Play a video game
121. Roast a roast
122. Put on a poncho
123. Catch Pokémon
124. Hold a balloon
125. Brush your teeth
126. Watch *Nailed It* on Netflix
127. Look into the sun
128. Read several jar labels
129. Throw a bag of potatoes into the ocean
130. Do the hokey pokey
131. Parallel park a car
132. Cross the street
133. Wave at a fire hydrant
134. Try on shoes
135. Stop a crime
136. Write a song
137. Put on a sweatshirt
138. Bench-press a baby
139. Trip a bitch you been beefing with
140. Golf
141. Change a tire
142. Press your nose on a widow
143. Parasail
144. Clean a window
145. Hug a widow
146. Hammer a nail
147. Sit in a hot tub and spill the tea on all your neighbors
148. Give directions
149. Wear Crocs
150. Play on a Slip 'N Slide
151. Get hurt on a Slip 'N Slide
152. Blow a kazoo
153. Snap
154. Learn all the choreography to the "Cell Block Tango" from the motion picture version of *Chicago*
155. Text a love interest you shouldn't
156. Learn about IRAs and pensions
157. Skip with a stroller
158. Dance like there are bees in your butt

159. Drink a milkshake
160. Ask the boys to leave the yard
161. Scratch a record
162. Point at a bitch stealing your style
163. Yell directions at an old person
164. Learn Spanish
165. Smile at a chicken
166. Flip off a cop
167. Cry for no reason at all
168. Tell your friend why they mean so much to you
169. Lie in the sand
170. Sit on a yacht and feel rich
171. Watch your creepy neighbor
172. Put your hair in an updo
173. Slide your feet into sandals
174. Do a backbend
175. Pack all of your belongings into a suitcase
176. Be a limo driver who becomes head coach of the New York Knicks
177. Eat two bowls of cereal with the same milk
178. Wag your finger at a dog
179. Wag your finger at your sexual partner
180. Put on a denim jacket
181. Count to thirty
182. Tickle a pig with a feather
183. Wake your friend up from a nap
184. Unpack all of your belongings
185. Text an aunt
186. Dig two holes
187. Scramble eggs
188. Eat a bowl of ice cream and then a bowl of fruit

189. Walk several dogs
190. Put on sunglasses
191. Get under a blanket
192. Surf a nasty-ass wave
193. Walk down a juicy trail
194. Hug your sister
195. Climb a mountain and jump into a waterfall
196. Greet the mail carrier
197. Go undercover in a convent with nuns and help the choir achieve stardom while also putting them in danger
198. Swing dance
199. Be happy

There are eighteen more things you can do in a bikini, but I didn't want to list them all. However, I want you to list ten things you can and will do in a bikini. If you post this list to Instagram, tag it with #veryfat #verybrave so I can see your #bravery!

1.

2.

3.

4.

5.

6.

7.

8.

9.

10.

Tips on Making Your Self-Esteem #Brave Like Your Bikini Body

1. Whisper to yourself (I say "whisper" so people don't think you've lost ya marbles) while in the bikini, "I'm a badass bitch. Every body is a different body; the one I have now is amazing. If I want to change it, I can, but for now, this is it, and this is perfect."
2. Wear bikinis often.
3. Take pictures in your bikini.

Tips on Taking the Most Flattering Picture of Your #Brave Body

Oh fuck, I don't have a tip for this! Ack! Fuck, sorry. Any picture of yourself is flattering. Fuck good sides and angles—enjoy every bit of yourself. Remember, if you don't like what you see, you can change it, but, baby, I bet what we get to see is amazing.

Tips on What Bikini to Pick for Yourself

1. Figure out what your favorite color to wear is.
2. Figure out if you like solids or prints.
3. Put that patterned or solid bikini on your body.
4. Look at yourself in the mirror. Do you like it? If you like it, that's your bikini!

Tips on How to Accept Your #Brave Body

My tip on accepting your #brave body is to realize that you only have one body, so why shouldn't you accept it? Easy, right? Now that you have accepted your body as #brave, I want you to go up to a mirror in your home and completely disrobe. I want you to look at your newly #brave body in the mirror. I want you to jiggle your fat and scream, "I AM A #BRAVE MOTHERFUCKER AND I'M ABOUT TO FUCK SHIT UP!" If you are not home alone you may scare whoever is home, but I think that's okay . . . sometimes people need a scary surprise.

Like, you may think that having this picture taken from a not-selfie angle is bad, but I look good as fuck! Fucking drink in all this #bravery.

Tips on Overcoming Skinny Influences in the Media

While representation of body diversity in media is changing, it's not changing fast enough. There is a deficit of different kinds of bodies in our current media landscape, and it has to evolve to represent all the bodies in the world. We're not there yet, obviously, so a good way to combat being constantly bombarded with thin images is to take a deep breath and understand that thinness is not some sort of objective standard of beauty. And don't get it twisted, I'm not saying thin is bad. It's not. What's bad is the concept that thin is the one, true ideal. But whose ideal? And not all ideals are truth. Some of those thin people aren't attractive to everyone. And besides, your worth isn't dictated by whether someone's attracted to you. So take a deep breath and realize your body is beautiful just the way it is. Then close the magazine or turn off your phone and live your #brave life.

Tips on How to Celebrate Your #Bravery

You ever throw a party? Throw one specifically at the beach or a pool. Any pool will do, public or private. Gather your friend/s and/or loved one/s, put on a bikini, and party. If you drink, bitch, get some rosé; if you don't drink, put some water on ice and feel your opulence. Oooh, baby, you better get a wireless speaker and play some music, 'cause bitch, this is a party. What I'm saying is, have fun in your bikini!

Tips on How to Make Your Other #Fat Friends #Brave

1. Look your fat friend in the eye and sit them down.
2. Say, "Brenda, I wanna take a step in our relationship. I wanna see your body." (Brenda may resist, and this may make them uncomfy, but talk Brenda off the ledge. Tell Brenda this isn't, like, a naked thing, it's a #bravery thing.)
3. Tell Brenda you want to go to a beach or pool situation with them and you want to see them in a bathing suit.

4. Let Brenda know that they don't have to be full-on #brave at first and they can wear a one-piece. #Bravery comes in steps.
5. When Brenda joins the beach or pool situation, tell Brenda how cute they look and then have a fun time being #brave together.

Tips on Dealing with "Chub Rub"

Wow, this one is tough, but if you google "chub rub," you will find so many solutions. There are lotions and gels galore! Also, you can wear bike shorts and take them off to swim. (If your belly is showing, remember you are still #brave.) If you don't know what "chub rub" is, well, well, well, isn't that nice for you. It's just a cute way of saying, "Ooooh my thighs rub together, they on fire! It hurts I'ma die."

Tips on What to Do When You've Really Exhausted the One Bikini You Have

There's only one thing you can do. Bitch, head back online or to the store and buy a new one!

Tips on How to Take Pictures of Yourself in Your Bikini for Social Media

Taking pictures is easiest if you have a fat friend or a thin friend to take the picture for you. Also, if you are in public you can ask a stranger to take it. Strangers love taking pictures for other people, because then they are the hero, and people love being heroes! Remember to ask for their Instagram handle so you can tag your hero. People love being heroes, but what they love more is to be tagged on Instagram (that's probably the thing people love the most). Also you can carry a selfie stick, but sometimes it's hard to capture all of your #bravery from that angle.

Tips on Wearing a String Bikini

I love a string bikini, because sometimes you feel like it may slide right off because there's so much of you and so little of it. But this is a situation where your fat is very #helpful. Just sit the string right in between a roll and that roll will #help hold that shit up.

#Bravery in a One-Piece Bathing Suit

You're not there yet, but baby steps, my li'l fatty.*

Tips on How to Work Up to Wearing a Bikini

1. Wear the one-piece.
2. Cut it in half.
3. Realize that won't work and now nothing will hold the suit up or keep it on.
4. Buy a bikini and never look back.

---

* Unless it's a one-piece with the middle cut out—that's #brave and I'll allow it.

BEHIND THE
#BRAVERY

Alright, it's time to fess up . . . come clean . . . tell the truth . . . Oh no! Here it goes!

I haven't always been #brave.

Fuck, that hurt. It hurt to tell you as your fearless, fat, #brave leader that I haven't always been this way. It took awhile for me to become the #brave bitch I am today. But although it was a long journey, I made it. I'm here and I'm extremely fucking #brave. I started off the way most people do: as a baby. Then, I became a child, then a teen, and now I've blossomed into a full-grown millennial. Let's start with when I was a baby, shall we?

BABY #BRAVE NICOLE

I was undeniably #brave as a baby. I ate whatever the fuck I wanted whenever I wanted to. If I wanted food and it wasn't out for the taking, I would just scream until someone gave me food. Badass and #brave, I know. I walked around in just a diaper with my fat li'l baby boobs sloshing around for the world to see. #Brave. I didn't care if my stomach showed when I raised my arms. #Brave. I wore tank tops, which is clearly ballsy, because a lot of fat women have a problem with their batwing arms. NOT ME. #Brave. I would say this period of my #bravery lasted about two years. Because after two years, I was a toddler and no longer a baby.

CHILD #BRAVE NICOLE

As a child, I was constantly told that I was too fat, and I would get upset but then quickly get over it. I'm assuming this is because I had undiagnosed ADHD (which I discovered recently as a grown millennial), so I never truly focused on it the way that other people did. In school, I had other shit to worry about besides my weight, like rushing through my work to help the unfortunate dumb kids who didn't know how to do anything right. Or starting a riveting conversation with my teacher about the trials and tribulations of being an eight-year-old. I don't really have memories of other kids at school making fun of me or anything like that. Maybe it's because I was a very loud kid who was friendly and funny, or maybe it's because I was one of only two black kids in my town, and the town didn't want all the diversity to get scared away. I don't know! I DON'T KNOW! All I know is that the other kids were mostly nice, *except* in gymnastics class. One girl called me fat, and I'll never forget it.

I regret not being #brave at this point in my life, because if I had been #brave, I would have had a comeback ready. Instead, I just agreed with her dumb ass and never went back to my gymnastics class. I didn't even have the #bravery to tell my mom why I quit. I just said I wasn't into gymnastics anymore, which was a bold-faced lie! I literally still love doing cartwheels, even though it kinda hurts my grown millennial body now. Having that little girl affect me to the point that I gave up something I enjoyed kills me. Who knows what I could have become if I had been #brave in that moment? I could have been a fat li'l Gabby Douglas!

I wish I could go back in time and whisper a comeback to little Nicole to say to that cunt. (Sorry if you took offense at my use of the word "cunt," but that's what that little cunt was acting like. Also, if you took offense, this probably isn't the book for you. I got some strong opinions and some real hot takes.) But, truly, to look at a joyful little black girl in a bright-blue unitard, cartwheeling and doing splits all over the gym—to look at her and say, "You're fat," knowing how much that would hurt her, that's what a cunt does. I would whisper to little Nicole, "Little Nicole, you look that li'l cunt right in her eyes and say to her, 'I know I'm fat, and that is okay. I'm also black, just in case you want to point out another obvious thing, and I'm happy as fuck, you rude motherfucker. While you were looking me up and down, waiting and thinking of something nasty to say to me, I was living my life and having the most fun. So go home and take a nap, ya cunt!'"

I forgive little Nicole for not speaking up, because it was before I truly found my #bravery. It was also before I discovered Ursula and Miss Piggy, who are badass fat bitches to look up to. Little Nicole didn't know that being fat is okay, because growing up, "fat" was a bad word, a nasty word. "Fat" was a word that could cut deep, take the air out of a room. My grandparents on my dad's side would encourage me to eat a second helping at dinner, but if I dared take a smidge too much, they would warn me that I was going to get "fatter than I already was," which was such a confusing mixed signal. (My relatives on my mom's side were pretty big eaters from the South, so with them I truly could eat to my heart's content and no one would say anything.)

Going to the doctor as a kid was also confusing. I'd get on the scale, and after the pediatrician made terrible jokes, he would very seriously turn to my mother and assure her that my "baby fat" would come off during puberty. Later, when it didn't, he'd make jokes about how I was going to be a late bloomer, and he'd tell me not to worry about that pesky "baby fat." I wish he wouldn't have called it "baby fat." I wish he had said, "You have excess fat. It's not baby fat, it's just regular-person fat. And you have two choices: enjoy it or change it. I'm a doctor, so here are some tools you can use to change it if you want, and if you don't want to use them, have fun and make sure you're healthy!" But, of course, no one gives you tools or useful advice when you're a fat kid. People seem to think that just reminding you that you're fat will magically change it. I personally have never done anything because someone just repeatedly told me to do it. I'm defiant like that. So why not try a different approach? Why not encourage kids to be the healthiest they can be in the body they choose to be in?

You may be reading this and thinking, "It's fucking simple: eat less, move more. Stop complaining about how hard it is for fat kids." Well, sure, I understand that now. Maybe if I'd found a sport I liked, I would have stuck with it. Maybe if I'd made healthier food choices, it would have stuck. Maybe if I'd made different decisions, I wouldn't have to be #brave. I could be a thin person worthy of living a life without people pestering me with their opinions about my body. But maybe I also wouldn't have to be #brave if we stopped defining people's bodies as anything other than just bodies.

TEEN #BRAVE NICOLE

As I got older, it got harder to brush off the fact that I was getting fatter than my older sister. It sucked not to be able to wear what she could wear. I loved clothes, and they didn't make much for girls my size. I would be so sad about having to shop in the "husky" kids' section of Sears. As a teen, I'd have to bypass the "juniors" section and head straight to the dusty corner of the store that housed the "plus-size" clothes. And then when I was trying on clothes, I had to deal with adult salespeople searching for a word instead of "fat" to describe how I looked in the clothes. I would try on girdles to stop my fat rolls from showing (girdles are evil and Spanx were invented to kill us all), and it was just an all-around unpleasant experience.

Then, my mom took me to Lane Bryant. I remember walking through their doors and feeling like I was in heaven, because they had so many options in my size. Sure, all the clothes were a little mature and a little too paisley for my sixteen-year-old tastes, but they were something I could work with. The store was honestly a true godsend (until I started working for them in my late teens, but that's neither here nor there—come to one of my live shows or watch my half-hour Netflix special "Aggressively Adorable," third episode of *Comedians of the World* thirteenth season, to hear me talk shit about that time in my life). I'll talk more later about being #brave while shopping. Promise and pinky swear.

One more thing about clothing #bravery here: I guess you could say I became #brave with my clothes during my teenage years, because as I expanded, my clothing options diminished. Sometimes I would get sick of Lane Bryant and the dusty, sad plus-size sections of department stores. So to compensate, I embraced clothing with spandex.

Spandex became my very best friend, because spandex allowed me to shop in the juniors' department. I also had li'l titties, which is oh so helpful for squeezing into clothing that doesn't truly fit you. You couldn't tell me that I didn't look good in my tight li'l dresses and tight li'l pants. Honestly,

I was walking around in skintight things LOVING MY LITTLE FUCKING LIFE. I adopted an attitude that was like *why the fuck do I care what other people think about what I'm wearing?* and I ran with it. Except when it came to bathing suits.

Man, bathing suits were truly my last hurdle with my own body acceptance, a.k.a. being #brave. At first, I would swim in a modest one-piece, and it was fine. Then as I got older and my friends hit puberty and got them nice titties and snatched waists, I got in my head about my own stunted titties and expanding hips and waistline. This caused my #bravery to falter, and I started to wear a shirt while swimming. Later, I added boy shorts after hearing the wind whistle through my friends' thigh gaps and then seeing my own thighs literally eating holes through my pants (my thighs are so hungry they eat all my pants). Then I started to wear straight-up pants in the pool. I would swim around, soaking wet in my own fucking clothing. And the dumbest part was that I knew I wasn't making myself look any thinner. I thought I was just sparing the world from having to look at my big dumb body.

Then little by little, I just stopped swimming altogether, which is very sad, because I love swimming. I'm a li'l water baby (read that in a high-pitched baby voice, because it's fun, and that's how I say it).

QUICK DETOUR BACK TO CHILD #BRAVE NICOLE

One of my earliest memories is of almost drowning in a pool. I was about four. I think I was in a children's swim class because my mother was determined to have my sister and I learn how to swim. Maybe she wanted to break the stereotype of black kids not knowing how to swim? It definitely wasn't in preparation to take a tropical vacation. Sidebar: we never went on a tropical vacation, even though my dad is from Barbados, because my mother would always say, "We'll go when I'm thin enough to wear a bikini." Spoiler: that never happened, but I still can't ask my mom why we took swimming lessons, because she's dead. What a bomb I dropped there.

Anyway, I was sitting at the edge of the pool, and our instructor was holding different kids, teaching them how to float. I was leaning over, trying to splash in the water with my hands, and I fell in. I remember the water washing over me and immediately opening my mouth to breathe and realizing that was a huge mistake. Then I remember thinking, "Oh fuck, I better do something different." By that point, the instructor had grabbed me and placed me back on the edge and frantically explained why we can't splash our hands in the water while we are sitting on the edge of the pool. Another sidebar: I was wearing arm floaties so it wasn't like I was gonna die or anything.

MILLENNIAL #BRAVE NICOLE

After that experience, it's weird that I don't have a fear of water. I guess the water didn't conquer me, so I decided to conquer it? I DON'T KNOW! All I know is I love swimming. I'm a li'l water baby (say it out loud like we did before), so it was a big deal when I made the choice not to go in the pool with my friends anymore. It was sad when I started to say, "Oh, I'll just have a drink by the pool," or, "Beaches aren't for me," or, "I hate the sun." (The third one is true—the sun is too hot sometimes. Like, for real, why are you being so bright and so hot? Can you chill out?) But later in my life, I was like . . . *the fuck*? There's not one reason why I shouldn't do the shit I enjoy. There's no reason not to throw on a bathing suit and live. So I bought a new bathing suit. Not a #brave one but a very dumb one, a swim dress from a Walmart in Kansas.

I was touring (doing improv, the #bravest form of comedy) with some friends, and a snowstorm stranded us in Kansas for an extra day. So we decided to have a pool day at the gross indoor pool in our gross hotel. However, I didn't have a bathing suit, and I knew my new bathing suit was going to have to be a bigger size than the last one I had bought, because I'd gained weight since my dad died. So we trekked over the hills of snow to a big, majestic Kansas Walmart to buy me a new bathing suit. And the only fat-size one they had was a swim dress. You know, a one-piece with a literal dress over it. So I bought that one.

That tour was wild, because I bought my first bathing suit since I was a teenager *and* I went to a strip club for the first time *and* got the world's most intense lap dance from a woman named Foxy. Okay, I'll tell you about that because it's about #bravery, even if it's not about fat #bravery.

QUICK DETOUR: A STORY ABOUT MY FIRST STRIP CLUB

Strippers are #brave in their own right, like sexually #brave and body-positive #brave. They take their clothes off for money (a thing people do every day for free) and get called whores by people. Some of those people are even the customers who frequent strip clubs (the gross level of hypocrisy in our world is astounding).

So anyway, here I was in Kansas with three friends (Callan, Bamanda, and Ravid*) who I performed comedy with at the Upright Citizens Brigade Theatre.

I can't remember who suggested we go to a strip club (let's get real, in all honesty it was probably, most likely, definitely me). The first one we found was a li'l grimy so we stayed for one beer and left. Then I Yelped another club, which I believe was called Baby Dolls (and if that's not what it was called, that's still what I'm gonna call it). Baby Dolls had a classic strip club vibe. A stage, a pole, and tables for patrons—you know, classic strip club!

We got our drinks and sat down. I clapped after each girl danced and tipped them each at least two dollars, because do they get a two-dollar base like a server, or do they make minimum wage? (I looked it up after I wrote that sentence, and I found out that a lot of strippers start out in the hole, so *they* have to tip out *the club* in order to dance there . . . *FUCKfuck*.) Anyway, good etiquette at a strip club or drag show is to tip at least a dollar or two or more per song. Not per girl—PER SONG. Also tip all the girls, even the ones you don't like, because liking a performance is subjective and arbitrary. Allot an extra twenty when you go; that's approximately how much extra after drinks you'll need to tip.

Anyway, girl after girl danced, and I was mystified by how they moved and how flexible and strong they were, pulling their body weight around that pole. Truly outstanding athleticism! And after their dances, each girl came over to our table to either sell a lap dance or to thank us for the tips, because apparently people don't realize YOU NEED TO TIP EVERY

---

* Not their real names.

GIRL FOR EVERY SONG, NOT JUST THE ONES YOU LIKE. Belladonna was a favorite. She had barbed wire tattoos all around her body, and she was the most athletic. She was also a little aggressive—when she found out that our table was there for the first time, she made Bamanda stand up and then sucked her nipple. Truly. Outstanding. I'm. Clapping. As. I'm. Typing. This. There was another stripper named Britney who had baby footprint tattoos and a '90s vibe. Then there was Barbie, who looked about eighteen, had pink spiky hair, and kinda told us too much about her home life. I hope she's okay.

Then there was Foxy. Oh man. Foxy I assume named herself Foxy as an ode to Foxy Brown, because she was a beautiful, badass black woman. During her dance, she made my friend Ravid stand up, and she grabbed a monkey bar hanging from the ceiling and swung her body straight into Ravid's head, wrapping her legs around his face. She wiggled around for a little bit and I've never seen a man happier. After her dance, she came over to our table and was funny and sexy. I think the whole table fell in love. Foxy taught us about the three different types of strippers.

Three types of strippers, according to Foxy:

Pole girls: girls who can do insane pole tricks.

Floor girls: girls who hump the floor and roll around.

Face girls: girls who are pretty and don't have to do anything.

I asked Foxy what she was, and she laughed and said "a face girl." It was true—she had only done a single trick and I was hooked.

So I decided we should all get lap dances. I'm 90 percent sure three out of the four of us got one. (Callan didn't get one out of respect to his wife, and now they have a baby. SEE, NICOLE, THERE ARE GOOD MEN OUT THERE.) My lap dance was fun and great until Foxy told me to sit back against the banquet. Then she stood above me, facing away from me with her feet on either side of my body and bent over, essentially sliding her vagina down my face before I could say, "That's okay, no thanks." It was the most intimate I've ever been with someone I wasn't being intimate with.

I loved that trip to the strip club so much that I started doing pole dancing. Also, maybe this seems like a long and unrelated tangent about a stripper's vagina, but I don't think it's a coincidence that after meeting someone so confident and #brave that she named herself Foxy, I put on a bathing suit for the first time in five years.

BACK TO THE GROSS INDOOR POOL IN KANSAS

To get ready for our gross indoor pool day inside our gross hotel, I flat-ironed my hair and put on makeup, because I'm smart and have perfect judgment. I guess my thought process was to make sure my face looked pretty if people were going to have to deal with seeing my body. When I arrived at the pool, my friends remarked how adorable I looked in my new swim dress, and I felt adorable too. I also felt foolish for all the times I was scared to wear a bathing suit and didn't have fun.

I wore the shit out of that swim dress. From then on I would get in the water whenever I could. I also cannot stress enough how stupid a swim dress is. As soon as you're waist-deep in water, the skirt part floats up around you like you're emitting a cloud of squid ink, revealing the thighs you are so desperate to hide. But I still wore it so at least, when I wasn't in the water, people wouldn't see things they didn't want to see. Until one drunken night in New Jersey.

That summer, I went to Paradise, a fantastic gay club in Asbury Park, New Jersey, with one of my best friends from high school, Snickolas Nervola.* We danced and drank our lives away. I vaguely remember getting White Castle and peeing in an alley. We ended up back at Snick's mom's house because she was away and her house has a pool. This li'l water baby (say it the way I want you to) was drunk, and this li'l water baby (do it again, it's fun) wanted to swim. I remember sitting with my feet in the pool with a stranger we brought home from the club—let's call him Carl because I truly couldn't tell you his real name. While Snickolas and Carl's friend were inside listening to music (and by listening to music I mean fucking), I sat there thinking, "I might as well swim in my underwear. I mean, that's kinda like a bikini." So that's what I did. I disrobed and dove in. If you're reading

---

* *Snickolas Nervola isn't his real name, but if you went to Middletown High School South around when I did, you know who I'm talking about.*

that correctly, you're realizing that this was the moment my #bravery was truly reborn. I disrobed in front of a stranger and swam. My first bikini was my underwear.

After that, I bought a bikini from Forever 21. But then, my #bravery temporarily halted. I guess it was halted by my sobriety? I had that bikini for a full year before I wore it. At that point, I had several different one-pieces, and I still had my trusty swim dress. I tried on that bikini several times and it definitely fit. It just didn't fit the way I was taught that a bikini should fit. I kept telling myself that I would wear it out when my stomach was a little smaller or when my thighs got a little slimmer. Then I took an impromptu trip to Palm Springs with my friend Marcy.* We booked a hotel with a fabulous pool, and I only packed bikinis. I thought to myself, "No one knows me in Palm Springs, I'll never see them again, who cares?!"

I had just bought a new car, but I made Marcy drive her old champagne-colored Chevy Cavalier. I don't remember my reasoning, and it's not important, but it's a nice detail. I got in her car and announced, "I only packed bikinis. I can't wait to take some nasty pictures and post them on Instagram. I'm going to hashtag them #veryfat #verybrave." Then we laughed and laughed for the entire two-hour drive and talked about how #brave we were going to be for the next two days. And that's how the second wave of my #bravery was born.

CURRENT #BRAVERY

So how #brave is Nicole now? I'm proud to say I am the #bravest I've ever been in my whole life. I have a pool at my place that I swim in pretty regularly. I wear all the tank tops showing my fat arms that I want. I wear a lot of belly shirts showing off that belly. And this year I decided to wear shorts more, because it's too dang hot to wear pants in the L.A. summer. I also found an activity that's changed my life.

I've always been impressed by strippers and pole dancers. Whenever I saw them dancing on Instagram or in person in clubs, I would be the

---

* Marcy is her real name.

loudest person cheering. I LOVE POLE TRICKS! When my friend Gilli asked a group of us to take a private pole-dancing workshop, I leapt at the opportunity. I took the class and had the best time—I was sore the day after but had so much fun. I didn't think about taking it up seriously until my very cool former assistant (now very cool friend), Eleanor, started to post on Instagram about her own pole dancing. I asked her where she was taking classes and, lo and behold, it was the same studio where I had taken that workshop.

I asked my best friend, Sasheer, to try a class with me, and she agreed. I asked for a friend to come with me because I previously had a terrible experience with group fitness, a disastrous Zumba class (truly whatta awful time I had). When a fat walks into a fitness class, they are often met with stares and the feeling like they don't belong. Not at this pole-dancing studio. This is pole, an already stigmatized form of fitness (Don't believe me? Ask the many dancers whose posts get taken down from Instagram, in a sort of shadow ban.), and they're more welcoming and open-minded as a result (in my opinion). My teacher, an amazing woman named Veronica, took the time to give me personalized adjustments and seemed to understand how my body moved better than I did.

When I first started going regularly, I would wear long shorts and a tank top, because I was scared to wear short pole shorts. Not because of my lack of #bravery but because I was intimidated by the athletes in my class and I didn't yet feel like I belonged in their league. One of the people who teaches and poles there, Ellyn, was instrumental in getting me out of my head. One day, I climbed my big #brave body almost to the middle of the twelve-foot pole, and when I slid down, she said, "Nicole, you are strong. We gotta get you in short shorts so you can grip the pole more." I scoffed, and she smiled and said, "No one cares. Also, you get to buy new stuff." She really got me.

I started to search hashtags like #plussizepole, and I loved what I found. I saw women of all shapes and sizes dancing in bikinis and tiny outfits. So I started dancing in tiny outfits too, because bare skin truly does make it easier to grip the pole and attempt the kinds of tricks I love. I'm not even remotely good, and it takes me longer to learn some of the moves, but each week I get better. It's always a real dream to get a move you've been working on.

I'm a year into doing it regularly, and pole dancing has made me realize how strong I truly am. Knowing the strength of your body is a real treat. I always knew I was strong. I threw shot put in high school, the ultimate fat girls' sport (people don't know this, but fat girls can sometimes help a track team win a meet—if it's close and you got a couple of fats in shot put, discus, and the javelin, you can win), but pole dancing made me want to get stronger. I started to work out more so I could attempt to do more aerial tricks, and now I almost can. I love pole, because every time I leave the studio, I feel very strong and like I've accomplished something tangible.

I truly wish someone—anyone—had said to me growing up, "Nicole, find a thing that moves your body that you also actually enjoy. Not to lose weight but to feel good. Moving your body can feel good." Doing pole doesn't make up for me quitting gymnastics, but it does feel really fucking good. I am #brave, but now that I've found pole dancing, I am also #strong and know my body better than I've ever known her before. And the people I pole with are the kindest, nicest people, who'll cheer you on when you climb higher or when you nail a trick you've been working on, and that support is truly so wonderful and inspiring. This sport and the people I do it with have made me #braver than I've ever been.

#Veryfat #verybrave: Look at three fat li'l Nicoles breaking all dem poles.

QUESTION:
You have so many bikinis! I'm poor and I would love to have tons of bikinis. What can I do?

ANSWER:
Mix and match, bitch!

Lemme explain a li'l bit more. A fun thing I do is buy solid-colored bottoms and mix and match the tops. Or the other way around.

It's a fun time and honestly saves so much room if you're packing for a sick-ass vacation. 'Cause, like, you can bring one bottom and like six tops.

MIX-AND-MATCH TIME!

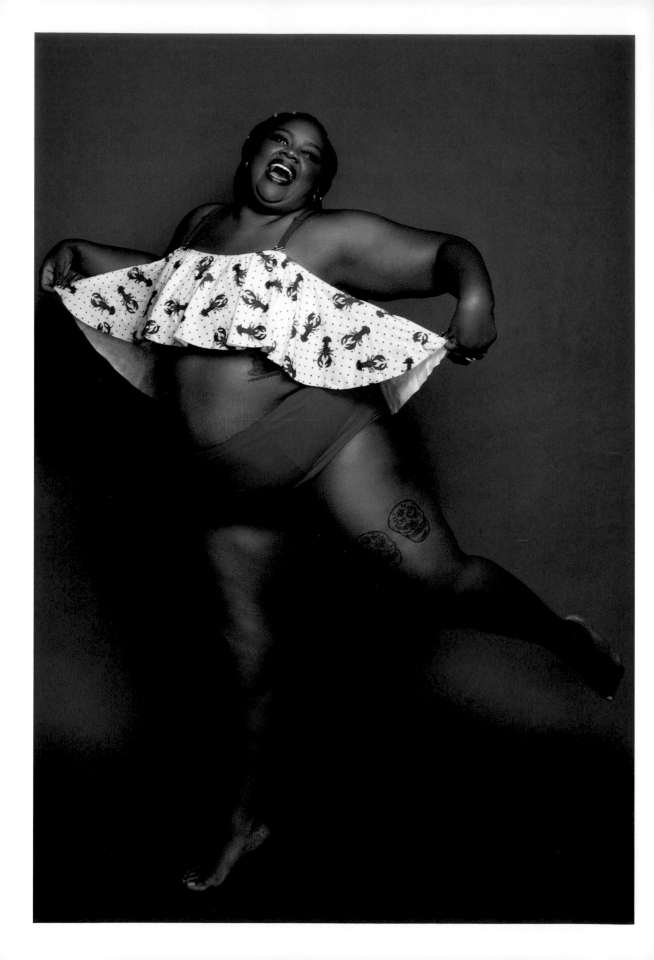

QUESTION:
Where the heck can I find bikinis?*

ANSWER:
Anywhere they sell them! You gotta try them on! If a store has plus sizes, they will probably have plus-size bikinis.

HOT TIP!

I love a deal, and I love getting exactly what I want. Say you find a bikini and the size you want is sold out. You can go to any resale website— eBay, Poshmark, or Etsy—and find exactly what you're looking for! Full disclosure: sometimes I look for things for years until I find them— it takes #dedication to get what you want. Remember, this goes both ways. If you have a cute bikini you don't wear anymore, list it on one of those sites to give it a new #brave home!

---

* This is a question I get asked ALL the fucking time.

#dontshophungry

Hey li'l fatties. I'll let you in on a secret. A bikini doesn't actually have to fit your body the way you thought it would fit your body for it to fit your body. I know you read that and got confused. You're like, "Bitch, if it doesn't fit my body the way I thought it was going to fit my body how will it fit my body in a way you think it's going to fit my body?" I'll tell you something: we've all collectively read and thought "fit my body" too many times. And your reward for reading and thinking about it is that I will tell you exactly what I mean.

But first: I know, sorry, you should know this happens with clothing too. You think something is too small and you don't even try it on because you've given up before you began. Now this isn't a foolproof plan, but it has helped me in the past and present, and it will help in the future, and I can't wait to share it with you. I know you're now thinking, "Bitch, you're stalling—give us the fucking bikini trick!" But, bitch, slow down—I have a word count I need to hit.

So anyway, I was in desperate need of a bikini with flames on it, because I fancy myself a little bit Guy Fieri-esque. I like to call myself Gal Fieri, because it's funny, but I also truly adore him. I once bought plane tickets so I could go on a date at Guy Fieri's airport burger joint, but that's a story for another time and for another book. Anyway, I had a hankering for a flame bikini to be #brave in and I couldn't find a traditional plus-size one. A lot of plus-size stuff I find is either too trendy or not trendy enough. Truly, it's devastating. I wanted a flame bikini, so I started to look at straight-size sites. I came across a very cool blue Moschino bikini with flames that looked airbrushed on it. I quickly ordered it and when it came I was a little worried that it wouldn't fit because I ordered their biggest size: large. But my good friend spandex came through for me again.

Now, when you post your #brave picture on social media you may get bombarded with comments trying to negate your #bravery. They may say things like, "That doesn't actually fit you." But let's get real. If it snaps, if it clamps, if it closes—it fits. It may show off ya rolls, bumps, and lumps, but guess what? That shit is there anyway, so why not show it off?

I'll let you know how this relates to other clothing too. I, for one, have very small titties, so if a shirt or a dress is stretchy I can probably get it on

'Cause that large fit my fat ass. To put it in perspective, I usually wear
a 3XL or a 22/24. ANYTHING IS POSSIBLE WITH SPANDEX!

my fat body. Will it look painted on? Probably. Will you be able to see the spandex in the fabric? Absolutely, but I like seeing the spandex because I know the shirt is doing its job by working hard to stay on my body. Also, when you can see the shiny spandex you look like you're glistening.

Side motherfucking ties . . . all you need for a bikini to "fit" is for it to cover your nasty bits that people don't like to see in public . . . front and top . . . tits and puss or whatever ya got . . . not my dang business.

I do have a disclaimer: this will not work all the time. Spandex isn't your every-time friend. Sometimes the spandex won't be enough to help you out. But that's okay; there are millions of pieces of clothing in this world. That said, this bitch doesn't give up that easy. I have another trick! Isn't that exciting? You can have a piece altered. You can buy two of those bitches, use one as the base and the other to put a panel on the sides, and BOOM, you have a cute li'l thang that is special and unique to you. I've done this with dresses and pants and bikinis, and sometimes it doesn't work out, but for the most part it does and I'm a happy li'l fattie.

That's it; those are the bikini tricks. Now to sum up:
1. Take a chance and try on something that may not be "your size."
2. Don't be upset if it doesn't fit.
3. If it fits (by covering your special private parts and staying on your body) or you can alter it to, wear the fuck outta it and be #brave.

This is an extra-large bathing suit. I am not an extra-large anything in clothing.

HOTTER TIP: If the string on the side isn't long enough, buy longer string.

Dealing with Insults

I understand that the world hasn't quite caught up to the #bravery in some women's/people's hearts and I do understand that there are wild motherfuckers out in the world who feel the need to tear people down publicly.

I've come up with some responses to insults people may throw at you. But I'll tell you this: just because someone throws something at you doesn't mean you have to catch it. What the fuck does that mean? It means just because something is said doesn't mean it's true. I go to therapy; does it show? Okay, on to the responses.

UNIVERSAL RESPONSE:

"Hi, I heard you! Thank you for your opinion. I just think it's funny that my body affected you so much that you needed to say something, while I've never thought about you and won't think about you again. I hope you wake up in the middle of the night and think about my big nasty body. I'll be sleeping soundly because you mean nothing to me. LOL, bye-skies!"

SPECIFIC RESPONSES:

INSULT:
You fucking cow!

RESPONSES:

"Moooo!" (To be perfectly clear, I want you to moo back at them.)

"You trying to milk me?"

"Yes, gorgeous to look at and tasty for some to eat."

"No, my name is Jan." (After you say that, follow them around, mooing.)

INSULT:
Wow, look at that whale!

RESPONSES:

"Is the whale okay? Because we are on land! Don't make me look at a dead whale!"

"I am not a whale, I am a cow! Mooooo!" This is inspired by Doja Cat's song, "Mooo!"

"Yes, I am majestic."

"Are you well? There's no whale anywhere."

INSULT:
Look at that fat ass.

RESPONSES:

"Yes, bitch, look at this fat ass!" Then twerk.

"WHERE IS THE ASS AND HOW FAT IS IT?" Start to twerk.

"Do I have to pull over?" Then sing Trina's "Pull Over" while twerking.

"Oh, thank you!" Then twerk.

"Sorry your ass is so small and no one looks at it!" Then get behind them, point at their small ass again, and say, "Such a shame you have a tiny stinky ass," while twerking.

INSULT:
Nasty fucking pig!

RESPONSE:

"Oink oink, bitch."

"That's what your dad calls me when he fucks me."

"I'm not a pig, I'm a cow, moooo! Wait, I'm not a cow, I'm a whale—wait, I'm Jan!"

"What's your name, Hillary Rude-ham Clinton!?"

"Pigs are cute; I'll take it!"

ANOTHER UNIVERSAL RESPONSE:

Cry. I know, I know, I know what you're thinking: Nicole, crying isn't #brave! To which I say, showing vulnerability is #brave. But I don't want you to really cry, I want you to burst into big ol' fake tears until they try to walk away. Then if they do walk away, chase them while crying. If they don't walk away and actually just apologize, I want you to stop crying and say, "Give me a fucking Oscar! I cannot believe you thought anything you have to say to me would actually matter. Hahaha you're a peasant!"

Now here's one more thing. If anyone calls you "crazy" for any of these responses, I want you to look them in the eye and say, "No, what's crazy is you thought it was okay to comment on my body. Worry about your own sad-ass life and fucking let a bitch breathe."

If you're feeling spicy, you can finish it off with a quote from Lil' Kim: "You know your mouth's a cage for your tongue if you just close your teeth."

Tips for the Allies, a.k.a. for the Nonfats Supporting Fats

There are a couple of things you can do to be helpful to your fellow fat friend. When trying to be supportive or complimentary on social media, avoid the following:

1. "You look thinner!" Unless the caption states they've lost weight and want to talk about it.
2. "Have you lost weight?" Unless the caption says something about it.
3. "Good angle!" All angles are good.
4. "You have a pretty face." You're implying the pretty face makes up for the fat body.
5. "You're almost there!" No need to tell someone that unless they're sharing a weight-loss journey; it's patronizing.

Honestly, any comment on social media about someone's appearance other than "you look wonderful" or a variation of that should be a crime punishable by jail.

Commenting on your friends' weight—don't do it. It's not your fucking business. Here's what you can do instead:

- You can ponder about it out loud alone at home.
- Gossip about it with another friend.
- Plan a dinner so you can see your friend in person, and if they wish to talk about their weight with you, great; if not, try step one or two again.

But other than that, it's not a compliment and not helpful. Because everyone looks good at every size they are.

VISUAL REPRESENTATIONS OF #BRAVERY

I took pictures of myself all around Los Angeles and captioned them with the worst-case scenarios that could happen while you're in a bikini. Just in case you still were wondering why wearing a bikini in public is #brave.

I am #veryfat #verybrave, but what if someone saw me outside in a bikini? There are only two trees here, and I would need more than two to cover my big body.

I am #veryfat #verybrave, but what if I stepped on that stair and it crumbled under the daunting weight of my nearly nude body?

#Veryfat and #verybravely showing off my new pig husband, who loves his curvy wife.

**#Veryfat and #verybravely riding my pig husband
(hoping he doesn't pop under the two tons of fun that is my body).***

---

* *I popped him two days later by accident. RIP, newly dead pig husband, and RIP being a curvy
wife.*

I am #veryfat #verybrave, because I'm showing the world how I have to drink water. I'm #veryfat, so I have to drink a lot of water to hydrate my big, nasty body, and the easiest way to do it is with a hose. Because they don't make cups big enough to quench my big #fat giant thirsty body. #veryfat #verybrave #secrets

#Veryfat #verybrave while watering the graveyard of plants I savagely ate because there was nothing in the fridge.

#Businessfat #businessbrave: Nothing will make a meeting go faster than exposing your fat ass to the boardroom. When you say, "Don't fuck with me, boys, this isn't my first time at the rodeo," everyone will know you mean it.

Ooooh, baby. I'm so #fat and so #brave wearing pineapples but drinking what I really want: a peanut butter milkshake treat with some other shit I can't remember. Very #brave to show the #belly and what's going into the #belly. #thirsty #thick

Double your pleasure, double your fun. Double the chins, double the fun!
Double the rolls, double the fun. Double the tittie sweat, double the fun!
Double the bellies, double the fun! Double the arm flaps, double the fun!
Double the #bravery! This is #veryfat #verybrave, because what if a small
woodland creature scampered into this backyard and saw these
twin chubby angels and lost its appetite?

Wow, this is real #bravery. What if my big, banging bod smashed all this tile, and the hot tub collapsed, and I crashed through the pool all the way through the layers of the earth, to the earth's core, and then I melted . . . slowly, because I have so much body. That's a lot of what-ifs. Truly so #brave to take that on. I commend myself.

Showing arms but still #notbrave

Oh, baby. This is #true #bravery. Standing in front of my favorite place in the house, pretending to be healthy by pretending to eat a banana while wearing a banana bikini. I love #pretending.

Did it hurt when I fell from heaven? Yeah, it did, because I fell out of the sky through a roof and tumbled down the stairs. And when big bodies tumble, people freak out because they think there's been a big earthquake. Also, a big, brown body in a brown bikini? WHOAH! What if someone walked in and thought my big body was a big dead body *and* it was naked? That would truly cause trauma for that person. SMDH.

Mmmmm . . . Raising my arms in a bikini is #brave. I'm showing off my bat wings. What if a gust of wind got caught in my arm flappers and I flew away?

#Thankgod I put my arms down.
It would have been so scary to take flight in my big body.

Look at this fancy-ass
bitch taking a #brave
picture next to a picture of
the same fancy-ass bitch.
Almost too much #bravery
for one picture.

Ahoy, friends! I'm about to show off my #bravery by sitting on this kid-size ATV and snapping it in half to make two separate motorcycles. Sorry not sorry about the damage—just being #brave here. Also #galfieri.

#Bravery doesn't know where or when it needs to be rolled in.

#Bravery is squatting a big body in a shopping cart while an old lady drives past, staring at you.

Sometimes I get so hungry I glug on gas. Diesel ONLY! If it's good enough for a semitruck, it's good enough for big, #brave me.

Such beauty and #bravery. What if a group of people wanted to play with this oversize chessboard? They would have to sanitize the whole board and all the pieces so they wouldn't catch a case of the fats. #veryfat #verybrave

Fat silliness? I mean, come on, this fat knee just pushing into this lounge chair is fully dangerous. Honestly, what if one of the hotel workers came out and saw me? They would be like, "Ew, a fat out in the open just lying on something another person would want to lie on? Also, she doesn't know how to lie in a lounge chair!" #veryfat #verybrave

My God, the #bravery here is stunning. A bikini with flames on it? What if someone thought I was a speedboat owned by Guy Fieri and rode me right into the ocean? What if a whale saw me and tried to wife me up?
#veryfat #verybrave

Kicking my leg up in the ocean? What the fuck am I trying to do, ladle out all the water with my big, scooping foot? I mean, California just got out of a drought. What if I kicked out so much water it caused a catastrophic tsunami? I would be the cause of so much damage—I would be the face of a preventable disaster! You are probably scared for me. "Nicole! You're standing in quicksand!" No, it's not quicksand, it's the weight of my poor food choices sinking me into the earth.
#veryfat #verybrave

In a bathroom in a bikini? What if I sat down on the toilet and broke it clean out of the wall?* #veryfat #verybrave

* I actually did this on June 15, 2019, a day I will remember forever.

Ronald McDonald forgot to order #bravery to go with the Happy Meal. #notbrave

Big Bertha and I have a lot in common. We both big as fuck, overdraw our lips, and like to be publicly fed. Two big bitches together is, say it with me: #veryfat #verybrave

This is a lady I don't know. She's in the book in case you needed a break from #bravery and fatness. This woman deserves to be in a bikini, but she is not #brave or fat. She's just exercising her right to be a thin, happy woman. If you flip the page, we get right back to the #bravery.

A tankini? Seems kind of #brave, but there's only a sliver of my stomach showing. That's why I'm standing next to a taxi. I'm going on a one-way trip to #brave town.

Look at this public display of #bravery*. I found two thin, fully clothed strangers and made them take a picture with me. They asked before the picture whether I was hungry and whether I was going to eat them. I laughed and said, "No, I just ate a child on the Ferris wheel, so I'm good for the next fifteen to twenty minutes."
#veryfat #verybrave

---

*This is the first bikini I ever bought. #historic

#Verycute #verybrave: Look at me eating what I love most: whipped sugar with food coloring. What if someone saw me and preemptively gave me an insulin shot without even asking if I needed it?

Look at this bitch, rummaging through the dumpster, looking for scraps of food like a fat li'l raccoon. I get it; wearing pizza on a bathing suit may seem #brave, but it's a one-piece. Maybe after recycling, it will come out as a bikini and finally be #brave.

#whatsexercise

#sittingburnscalories

It's #verybrave of me to lie to the world at the iconic Muscle Beach Gym. We all know I'm not a gym rat; I eat rats.

Making eye contact with people in the passing airplane. I'm so large, they can see every roll with clarity reserved for people #blessed with twenty-twenty vision. I'm also looking at all the thin, #notbrave birds in the sky. #brave

This is a misleading picture; you think it's #brave because we all know fat people only eat out of buckets with their hands no matter the genre of food. But this is a one-piece. #notbrave

Do I have to say it? I mean, what if this insanely huge, nasty body broke the fuck outta this Ferris wheel mid-wheeling? It would be devastating to all the families that thought the Santa Monica Pier was a cool, safe space for normal-size people. #veryfat #verybrave

A cute picture of me pretending to let a shark eat me, but let's get fucking real:
if I met a shark in the ocean, I would beat it to death first with my tit and then
eat it raw while I floated on my back. #veryfat #verybrave

#erotic

#sensual

#Veryfat #verybrave: It's incredibly #brave to bring what turns me on to the beach. Most people wouldn't dare bring erotica to a public place. Not me; I want all of the beach people to watch me roll around on a donut towel to a climax of excitement of the anticipation of eating an actual donut.

Wow, such #bravery eating ice cream where a child might see me!
What if one of those children looked at me and thought it was okay to be #fat?
#yum #fattyfun

This is an outrageous display of #bravery. What if I tumbled down this hill
and murdered everyone in Los Angeles with my thunder thighs
and #MASSIVE #BELLY?

Dang, podcasting is #verybrave, especially as a #woman. But as a #fat #woman? I mean, what if listeners of my podcasts *Why Won't You Date Me?*, *Best Friends* with Sasheer Zamata, *Drag Her!* with Mano Agapian (currently available wherever you can get podcasts), and *90 Day Bae* with Marcy Jarreau (a recap podcast of *90 Day Fiancé*, available only on Patreon) heard my heavy breathing? What if they found out I got winded sitting down? #brave

Pretending to surf? Yeah, right, we all know that the board would just snap in half in real life . . . #delusional #brave

#Bravely trying to make friends with something that might not know I'm fat.
Shhh, they know.

'Bout to crush this tile with my ham hock hands.
#bravely #demolishing #buildings

#Bravery is staring down all the ants on the sidewalk that quake with fear, anticipating your next movement.

#Bravery is finding furniture in nature to support your weight. #fuckflimsyplasticchairs

Fat people are *never* in fast-food commercials, because fat people eating fatty foods makes everyone go crazy. So, standing outside a fast-food place, eating fast food in a bikini? #Bravery. Truly, what if everyone eating inside saw me and started to puke everywhere?!

A thin man is taking a picture of this #bravery to alert his family that a fat moved in next door. Also, walking outside in nature at this size? With three dogs? #Brave confession: I ate the other dog. Me so hungry.

#Bravery is walking around a construction site; each fat step I take knocks down two things they built.

#Verybrave: This used to be one big rock, but I twerked my big butt on top of it, and it crumbled into a million little rocks.

Oh, wow, you could be a "babe," but you're just a dumpster bitch. #onepiece #notbrave
Babe
TRASH HERE
TRASH HERE

Sometimes you take a photo next to a store with a famous wall, and they say, "NO PROFESSIONAL #BRAVERY ALLOWED," so you change in your car and sneak another picture, but farther away from that wall, while still keeping that wall in the background.

About to smash this banana in my tummy. #verybrave

Sitting on nothing but string strung together is maybe the #bravest thing a fat can do.

#Bravely touching these statues. What if they crumbled under the weight of my hooflike hands?

Keep sipping; maybe you'll drink in enough #bravery to be #brave. Until then, #notbrave.

#enjoyingbravery

Very #brave of me to shower #bravely with the door unlocked.
Pretty sure the person who walked in was more scared.

I kept saying, "Ooh, look, a sports center, and I'm wearing a sports hat!"
Turns out, I'm wearing the wrong sports hat, but I couldn't hear because of
all the fat clogging my ears. #verybrave

#Veryfat #verybrave: What if a child saw me in the pool and tried to mount me like an inflatable toy? Then I would have to speak to the child and let them know that while I am buoyant, I am not a toy. I am #brave.

I am #veryfat #verybrave wearing my bikini in a hotel pool! What if other hotel guests saw me and got sad? What if they decided never to return to the hotel again because of the fatty infestation? What if other fat women thought it was okay to do the same thing?! What if my big body tumbled into the pool and all the water splashed out? #veryfat #verybrave

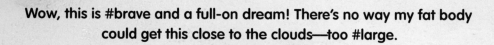

Wow, this is #brave and a full-on dream! There's no way my fat body could get this close to the clouds—too #large.

Another break from #bravery. This time, we have three thins to palate cleanse your eyes from all the fat.

This is #brave—an elephant-size woman sitting on wicker?
A disaster waiting to happen.

#Bravely showing off the size fork I need to shovel food into my gaping mouth hole.

ONE WAY TO FEEL #BRAVE* IN A BIKINI IS TO BOOK A STUDIO AND HAVE A PHOTO SHOOT.

---

* The captions are still worst-case scenarios.

Green! Yellow! Orange! Wow, so many #brave colors. I'm out here looking like a nasty li'l highlighter for all of your assignments, like eating.

#Verybravely found out these fake lemons aren't tasty. Please stop making fake food look real, 'cause I get duped every time.

What's #brave? Eating your own finger 'cause you're hungry.

#Bravery is trying to balance all this fat while wearing peppers on your bathing suit top, when everyone knows you don't eat veggies.

I've never seen a fat zebra! I guess anything is possible! #veryfat #verybrave

This is pretty #brave, showing my big butt to a photographer. What if my fat butt made the photographer sick, and they passed away? #bigzebraenergy

This is #verybrave, just because of personal safety. What if I flipped right over and landed on the floor and broke my neck? #brave

#MarilynMonFATroe

#Bravery is pretending to be a pinup knowing fully well you couldn't ever be pinned up to anything.

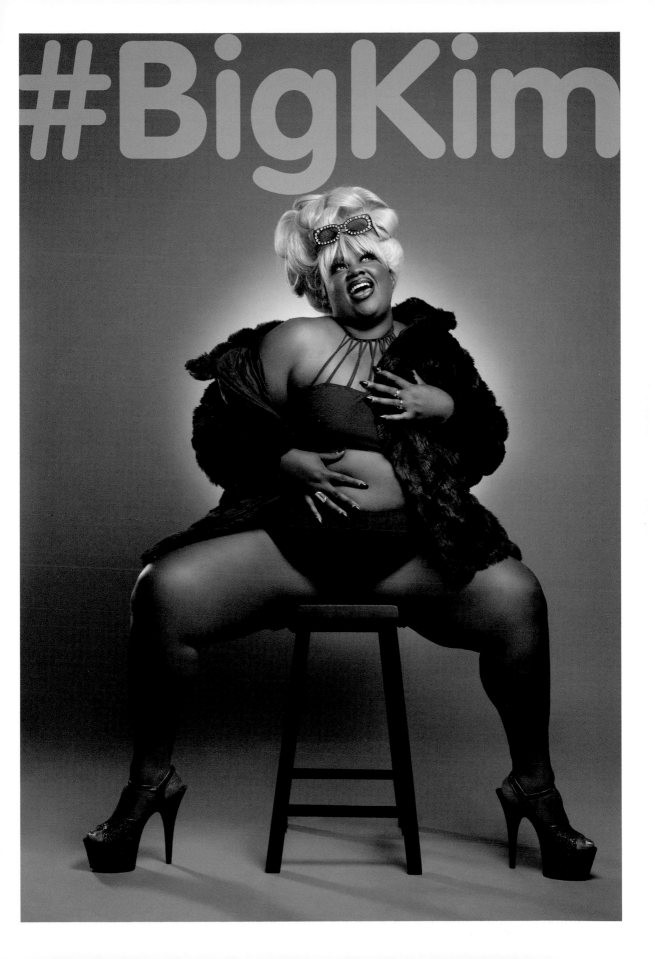

#BigKim

#EnormousK.I.M.

#VeryFatVeryBraveKim

#GargantuanKim

#NotoriousB.I.G.

#HotCheetoMouthPour

#Bravery is wearing bikini bottoms that are clearly too small for all dat #ass.

#Bravery is squatting in heels. What if my knees said "it's a wrap" and popped outta my body?

#bigbutt

You think this is the same bathing suit as the one before, but it's not.
Name the things that are different in the space below.

1.

2.

Answers: 1. The top is different. 2. The bottom is different.

159

These braids are very long and heavy. #Bravery is adding more weight to your overweight body.

#Bravery is being fat and wearing fur anything. The photographer might think I killed and ate a rabbit and kept the fur for a foot decoration. #brave

Wow, sitting on any store-made piece of furniture is #verybrave.
I've broken toilets, so I can probably break this stool. Risking breaking
furniture takes real #bravery.

#Gravity would never allow this. #veryfat #verybrave

Wishing upon a star for snacks.

#Bravery is pretending to touch your toes.

Wearing a bikini with a UFO on it is #brave. I say it's #brave because we all know that a fat could never be abducted. The sheer weight of my insanely huge body would keep me #tethered to the ground.

I'm making a list, and I'm checking it twice, because if I go to the grocery store, then get home and realize I forgot the entire cake I planned on eating for dessert, I'll be on my own naughty list. #brave

Looking to cause a tornado with the velocity of my hugely overweight spins. #brave

Earth. Wind. Water. Fire. Candy. Ice Cream. Cookies. Lasagna. Mashed Potatoes.
Calling on the nine elements of the earth. #brave

("Behind the scenes," a cool Hollywood term)

just wanted to check in with you guys. I know you've been looking at a lot of pictures, thinking, *Okay, wow, so she truly used the same wigs, and her shoes are the same in a lot of these pictures*. Yes, this is true. I had limited time and resources, and by resources, I mean money. If I had more money, I would have used a stylist, a hair and makeup team, and a professional location scout, but #bravery doesn't come from money, it comes from the heart, and so does this book.

Since Kim and I took all these pictures by ourselves in six days and with a *very* loose plan, I had to change my bikini in public numerous times. It was very interesting to see the responses I got from people in the wild who saw me either in my bikini or changing into my bikini on the side of the road.

Men: Overwhelmingly catcalled, yelled, and truly couldn't control themselves. Some of the men were with women who didn't say anything, which I found interesting. When men drove past me, they would *break* their necks trying to look at me. Men seem to gawk at all women as if they are the first one they've ever laid eyes on. I even had one man grope me. He slapped my ass, which wasn't very cool. You're probably thinking, "Nicole, how did this happen?" I'll tell you: it happened when I wandered onto a construction site with Kim to take some of these photos. And I bet now you're thinking, "Well, Nicole, you did wander onto his construction job site unannounced in a gold lamé bikini." To you, I say, okay, maybe I shouldn't have snuck in, but me sneaking into a place where I shouldn't have been isn't an invitation to touch me in any way . . . It was shitty, but it just reminded me—served as a warning that men are going to lose their minds getting used to all this #bravery. It sucks, but then a lot of men suck. I have a tip on dealing with unwanted touching. You know how we tell children to yell if a stranger touches them? We gotta do the same when a dude oversteps his bounds. Get loud and embarrass the fuck out of him.

Women: They were usually either silent or gave a warm smile. One lady actually said, "Oh, wow, you look so good!" which I liked. It felt nice to receive a compliment in a civilized way. This is not to say that women are better than men but . . . on the whole, they definitely are.

As Kim and I slaved though all the pictures of me in bikinis, Kim asked me two questions: "Are you tired of looking at yourself?" and "Do you have a new perspective of yourself?"

My answer to the first question was: well, I love looking at myself; I'm a very vain person. I think I'm pretty, and if there is a mirror, I will look at it. That's not to say that I don't look in the mirror sometimes and think, *Yuck, what a dumpster bitch*, because I do. I have good days and bad days. But a lot of the time, I choose to like what I see, and a lot of times it's not a difficult choice. I genuinely love me, and I hope that other people will learn to love themselves as well, hopefully by the end of this book. I will say this: after looking at my body in pictures of all different angles, I do think I love my physical body more. Like, as a whole. Which is why one of my tips is to look at yourself naked in a mirror. Repeatedly looking at my body and really appreciating looking at it has been a lovely experience.

As for the second question, I'm not sure I have a new perspective on myself. I think it would be hard for me to love myself MORE. However, I used to be shy about changing in front of people and now that's fully gone. During one of our shoots I was changing and fully had my pussy out while Kim was in the room, and she didn't care and neither did I. Bodies are bodies.

Kim didn't ask me this, but I want to address a question I get a lot: "How did you get your confidence?" And I guess I've more or less just decided life is already really fucking hard and I don't want to spend it hating what I see in the mirror. It took me awhile to get here, so I'm writing this book so another fat li'l fatty somewhere can choose to love themselves too. Because the world can be cruel, so why not at least be nice to yourself?

So be #veryfat #verybrave and go out and terrorize the world with your #bravery. You can literally substitute a bikini for anything you're scared to do. I just want you to know that only you stand in the way of you. I truly hope that this book inspires people—big, small, male, female, nonbinary, trans, and everyone in between—to live their best lives, their happiest lives.

Tips for the Rest of Your Life

1. Love the body you're in. Remember, most of us can change what we don't like, and if you can't change it, that's okay. You are perfect.
2. Move your body, not to lose weight but to feel those endorphins . . . it's real. If you cannot move your body, do things that make you feel good and accomplished.
3. Look at yourself naked often.
4. *this one is really hard* Speak to yourself in a nice way.
5. If you need help, reach out. Therapy is great, and medication if you need it can help.

Now I want you to write down three things you're going to do every day to make yourself feel good in your body. It truly can be as simple as remembering to put on lotion every dang day.

1.

2.

3.

Yup, the end.

OKAY, BYE-BYE!

About the Author

NICOLE BYER is an actress, comedian, writer, producer, podcaster, and a nice person. Nicole hosts the Netflix baking show *Nailed It!* and had a sitcom (RIP), *Loosely Exactly Nicole,* on Facebook Watch. She also hosts many a podcast: *Why Won't You Date Me?, Best Friends* with Sasheer Zamata, *Drag Her!* with Mano Agapion, and *90 Day Bae* with Marcy Jarreau. You've seen her on MTV's *Girl Code, 30 Rock, The Good Place, Brooklyn Nine-Nine, A Black Lady Sketch Show*, and in a Nestlé commercial that only runs in Israel. Her half-hour stand-up special, "Aggressively Adorable," is featured on the Netflix series *Comedians of the World*. You can hear her voice on *Tuca & Bertie, Bob's Burgers*, and *Big City Greens*. Nicole has done lots of fun shit. She also tours the dang country, so go see one of her shows! She lives in Los Angeles with one JoÚ Milhiser and two fun dogs. She's currently looking for a boyfriend.

Andrews McMeel Publishing
a division of Andrews McMeel Universal
1130 Walnut Street, Kansas City, Missouri 64106

www.andrewsmcmeel.com

www.nicolebyerwastaken.com

20 21 22 23 24 TEN 10 9 8 7 6 5 4 3 2 1

ISBN: 978-1-5248-5074-6

Library of Congress Control Number: 2019950001

Editor: Allison Adler
Art Director: Holly Swayne
Production Editor: Elizabeth A. Garcia
Production Manager: Tamara Haus
Photographer: Kim Newmoney

Attention: Schools and Businesses
Andrews McMeel books are available at quantity discounts with bulk purchase for
educational, business, or sales promotional use. For information, please e-mail
the Andrews McMeel Publishing Special Sales Department:
specialsales@amuniversal.com.